D0325915

Laugh
Your
A**
Off

Jack Kreismer

RED-LETTER PRESS, INC.
Saddle River, NJ

LAUGH YOUR A** OFF
COPYRIGHT ©2018 Red-Letter Press, Inc.
ISBN-13: 9781603871587
ISBN: 1603871586

All Rights Reserved
Printed in the United States of America

Red-Letter Press, Inc.
P.O. Box 393
Saddle River, NJ 07458

www.Red-LetterPress.com

Introduction

A Vanderbilt University study found that laughing intensely for an hour could burn as many calories as lifting weights for 30 minutes.

Dr. Helen Pilcher, who has a PhD in biology and has dabbled in comedy, knows a thing or two about funny business. Her research has shown that laughter can burn 120 calories per hour. It also boosts blood flow, she says, which makes for a cardiovascular workout as well!

Medical doctor Madan Kataria, the founder of Yoga Laughter Clubs, thinks there's nothing like a good, healthy, har-de-har-har as he said, "I have not seen anyone dying of laughter, but I know millions who are dying because they are not laughing."

So go ahead- Laugh Your A** Off!

Jack Kreismer

ACKNOWLEDGMENTS

BOOK DESIGN & TYPOGRAPHY:
Jeff Kreismer

•

COVER ART:
Design by Damonza

•

EDITORIAL:
Jeff Kreismer

•

CONTRIBUTORS:
Russ Edwards
Kobus Reyneke

•

DEDICATED TO:
Uncle Al Salerno

THE LAUGH YOUR A** OFF MENU

Laugh Your A** Off

Laugh Your A** Off

Laugh Your A** Off

A Man Walks Into A Bar...

Bottoms up as you begin to burn off that bottom with these belly busters.

A fish walks into a bar. The bartender says, "What would you like?"
The fish gasps, "Water!"

....

A bowl of cornflakes walks into a bar. The bartender says, "Sorry, we don't serve breakfast here."

....

A bishop walks straight into a bar. The bartender says, "You can't do that. Bishops can only move diagonally."

You know you're on a diet when cat food commercials make you hungry. -Andy Bumatai

DRINKS

Bartender: "I see your glass is empty. Would you like another one?"

Customer: "Why would I want two empty glasses?"

= = =

A guy stepped up to the bar and ordered a martini. Before drinking it, he delicately removed the olive from the glass and put it into a small jar he took from his pocket. After downing the drink, he ordered another and again took the olive from it and placed it into the jar. He repeated this process several times until the jar was full of olives. He then paid the bar tab and staggered out.
A customer who saw what had gone on said to the bartender, "Boy, that was really weird."
The bartender answered, "What's so odd about that? His wife sent him out for a jar of olives."

= = =

Two guys are at a bar. The first one gloomily says, "I drink to forget. How about you?"
The second guy nods and says, "Me too. Why do you drink?"

You can't lose weight by talking about it. You have to keep your mouth shut. -Farmer's Almanac

Q: Why do elephants drink?

A: It helps them forget.

= = =

Julius Caesar walks into a bar, holds up two fingers and says, "Five beers, please."

= = =

After the little pig had downed ten beers, the bartender said, "I bet you'd like to know where the bathroom is."

"Nope," answered the pig. "I'm the little pig that goes wee-wee-wee all the way home."

= = =

A guy notices a seal sitting across the bar from him. The seal says to the guy, "Hey, that's a great haircut you have. What a nice smile you have, too. And that jacket fits you to a tee. You're looking terrific, buddy."

The guy says to the bartender, "What's that all about?"

The bartender says, "That's the seal of approval."

You can only hold your stomach in for so many years.
-Burt Reynolds

DRINKS

Maybe you've heard the one about the guy whose doctor told him to eat more vegetables. Now he puts three olives in his martinis.

===

A brain walks into a bar and the bartender says, "Sorry, I can't serve you."
"Why not?" asks the brain.
"You're already out of your head."

===

Two ten-dollar bills go into a tavern. The bartender says, "I'm sorry, but I can't serve you. This is a singles bar."

===

Charles Dickens: I'll have a martini.

Bartender: Olive or twist?

===

A penguin waddled into a bar and said to the bartender, "Was my dad here today?"
"I dunno. What does he look like?"

The perfect lover is one who turns into a pizza at 4:00 a.m. -Charles Pierce

A snake slithers into a bar. The bartender says,
"Sorry, we don't serve snakes here."
"Why not?" asks the snake.
"Because you can't hold your liquor."

■ ■ ■

Three fonts walk into a bar. The bartender says,
"Sorry, you'll have to leave. We don't want your
type here."

■ ■ ■

A guy walks into a bar with a roll of tarmac
under his arm and says, "A beer please, and
one for the road."

■ ■ ■

A guy walks into a bar and sees a horse serving
drinks. The horse asks, "What are you looking
at? Haven't you ever seen a horse tending bar
before?"
The guy says, "No, it's not that. I just never
thought the parrot would sell the place."

*According to a brand new scientific study, more than
90 percent of diet plans used by Americans do not
work. The American scientists conducted this study
by looking out a window. -Conan O'Brien*

An old geezer walks into a bar wearing a stovepipe hat, a waistcoat and a long, phony beard. He sits down at the bar and orders a beer. As the bartender serves him, he comments, "You look like you might be going to a costume party."
"You're right," says the old guy. "I'm supposed to come dressed as my love life."
"But you look like Abe Lincoln," says the bartender.
"Yep, that's right," says the old man. "My last four scores were seven years ago."

= = =

A dog walks into a bar and says to the bartender, "Hi, my name is Roger and I'm a talking dog. How about a drink for a talking dog?"
The unimpressed bartender says, "Sure, the toilet is right down the hall."

= = =

The past, present, and future walk into a bar. It was tense.

In the Middle Ages, they had guillotines, stretch racks, whips, and chains. Nowadays, we have a much more effective torture device called the bathroom scale.
-Stephen Phillips

DRINKS

A Red Sox fan walks into a bar in Boston and notices a guy wearing a Yankees cap. The Red Sox fan announces out loud to the bartender, "Drinks for everyone, except for that Yankee fan!"
The Yankee fan grins and says, "Thanks."
This irritates the Red Sox fan so he orders another round of drinks for everyone except the Yankee fan. Once again, the Yankee rooter thanks him. This continues for another couple of rounds until the Red Sox fan asks the bartender, "What's up with that guy in the Yankee hat? I order drinks for everyone except him and all he does is thank me."
"Indeed, he should," answers the bartender. "He owns the place."

...

A horse walks into a bar. The bartender says, "Hey!"
The horse says, "Sure."

...

Eight Canadian geese walked into a bar.
They ordered a V-8.

Your body is not the real you, it's just the meat you live in. I like that: it means that the real me doesn't really have a humongous butt. -Jessica Zafra

An amnesiac walks into a bar, goes up to an attractive blonde and says, "So do I come here often?"

* * *

A weasel walks into a bar. "You're underage," says the bartender. "I can't serve you alcohol, so what would you like?"
"Pop," goes the weasel.

* * *

A mummy walks into a bar. The bartender says, "What'll it be?"
The mummy answers, "Nothing. I just came in here to unwind."

* * *

A dog walks into a bar and asks the bartender, "Do you have a job opening?"
The bartender says, "Why don't you try the circus?"
The dog responds, "Why would the circus need a bartender?"

Probably nothing in the world arouses more false hopes than the first four hours of a diet. -Dan Bennett

A Waist is a Terrible Thing to Mind... And Other One-Line Calorie Burners

*This is the perfect stretching exercise for those smile muscles as you make your way into the Laugh Your A** Off workout.*

Vegetarians, if you love animals so much then why do you keep eating all their food?

Frosty the snowman was seen looking through the carrot bin at the supermarket. He was picking his nose.

Turning vegan is a big missed steak.

I, for one, like Roman numerals.

Food is like sex: When you abstain, even the worst stuff begins to look good. -Beth McCollister

Knowledge is knowing a tomato is a fruit.
Wisdom is not putting it in a fruit salad.

Two clowns are eating a cannibal. One says to
the other, "I think we got this joke wrong."

The world chess champion was having dinner
with his wife. There was a checkered tablecloth.
It took him two hours to pass her the salt.

A man walks up to a blind guy and hands him a
piece of matzo. The blind guy says, "Who wrote
this nonsense?"

If you ordered pasta and antipasta, would you
still have an appetite?

Did you hear about the new 12 step program for
people that talk too much? It's called
Onandonanon!

*When we lose twenty pounds, we may be losing the
twenty best pounds we have! We may be losing the
pounds that contain our genius, our humanity, our love
and honesty. -Woody Allen*

What do you call it when a chicken sees a salad?
Chicken Caesar salad

What do you call a fake noodle?
An impasta

What is green on the inside, white on the outside, and hops?
A frog sandwich

What do you get when you cross a turkey with a centipede?
Drumsticks for everyone

Why do cows wear bells?
Their horns don't work.

How does an elephant climb a tree?
He hides in an acorn and waits for a bird to carry him up.

I have gained and lost the same ten pounds so many times over and over again my cellulite must have déjà vu. -Jane Wagner

What should you do if you see a spaceman?
Park in it, man.

What goes "Ho ho ho, plop"?
Santa Claus laughing his head off

What does a Thesaurus have for breakfast?
A synonym roll

What did the pirate say when he turned 80?
"Aye Matey."

What do you call an eye doctor living on an
island in Alaska?
An optical Aleutian

Why did the invisible man look in the mirror?
To make sure he still wasn't there

What do you call two birds that stick together?
Velcrows

*The reason fat people are happy is that their nerves
are well protected. -Luciano Pavarotti*

What would you call the child of a vampire and a snowman?
Frostbite

What do you call an arrogant criminal going down stairs?
A condescending con descending

What do you call an Italian hooker?
A pasta-tute

What do you call a group of babies?
An infantry

What do you call a hippo without a butt?
A hippo-bottomless

What's a pirate's favorite letter?
P, because without it they're irate

Where do poor meatballs live?
In the spaghetto

A party without cake is just a meeting. -Julia Child

Why do scuba divers fall backwards off the boat? Because if they fell forward, they'd still be in the boat.

What do you call it when someone arrives at the cookout and realizes they forgot the ketchup?
Heinzsight

Why does Waldo wear stripes?
Because he doesn't want to be spotted.

What do you call a singing laptop?
A Dell

What do you call Dracula with hayfever?
The pollen Count

Do you know what gingerbread men have on their beds?
Cookie sheets

The only way to keep your health is to eat what you don't want, drink what you don't like, and do what you'd rather not. -Mark Twain

What's the fastest race car in the world?
A Fazool - Nobody ever pasta fazool.

What do you call an Amish guy with his hand in a horse's mouth?
A mechanic

What do you call a caveman who wanders aimlessly?
A Meanderthal

What did the Tin Man say when he got run over by a steamroller?
"Curses! Foil again!"

What do you call a person who makes allegations about reptiles?
An alligator

Why did Johnny Appleseed cross the road?
To get to the other Cider

It would be far easier to lose weight permanently if replacement parts weren't so handy in the refrigerator.
-Hugh Allen

APPETIZERS

What does Mother Rabbit say to the Easter Bunny when he leaves for work on Easter morning?
"Break an egg."

Why did the Pepsi executive get fired?
He tested positive for Coke.

What kind of street lamps do they have in Jerusalem?
Israelites

What do retired Naval officers and beached whales have in common?
Long time no sea

What do you call a nervous javelin thrower?
Shakespeare

What do you call a dinosaur with an extensive vocabulary?
A thesaurus

Health food may be good for the conscience, but Oreos taste a hell of a lot better. -Robert Redford

What do you call a fat psychic?
A four-chin teller

How is playing a bagpipe like throwing a javelin blindfolded?
You don't have to be very good to get people's attention.

Why do the French like to eat snails so much?
They can't stand fast food.

Why do lions eat raw meat?
Because they don't know how to cook.

What is a happy cowboy's favorite candy?
A Jolly Rancher

Why wouldn't the sesame seed leave the casino?
Because he was on a roll.

What kind of bagel can fly?
A plain one

I had a cholesterol test. They found bacon. -Bob Zany

APPETIZERS

What do you get if your sheep studies karate?
A lamb chop

Why did the rooster cross the road?
He heard that the chickens at KFC were pretty hot.

What did Sushi A say to Sushi B?
Wasabi!

Why do fish live in salt water?
Because pepper makes them sneeze.

What's the difference between an onion and a lawyer?
When you cut the onion, you cry.

I'd hate to be a member of Overeaters Anonymous. It's not like Alcoholics Anonymous where you can hear some wild testimony of drunken debauchery. How exciting can OA testimony be? It's not like you're ever going to hear, "Wow, I'm sorry...I was so full last night I don't remember meeting you." -Laura Kightlinger

"Waiter, There's a Fly..."

*Here we bring back one of the old staples
of the comedy menu with some consommé
punchlines to trim your waistline.*

Customer: "Waiter, there's a fly in my soup!"
Waiter: "Please be quiet, sir. Everyone will want one!"

"Waiter, I refuse to eat this roast beef. Please call the manager!"
"That's no use. He won't eat it either."

"Waiter, this soup tastes funny."
"Funny? But then why aren't you laughing?"

"Waiter, there's a fly in my soup!"
"That's alright, sir. He won't drink much."

To me, an airplane is a great place to diet. -Wolfgang Puck

soup

"Waiter, there's a fly in my soup!"
"Don't worry, sir. That spider on your bread will soon get him."

"Waiter, there's a fly swimming in my soup!"
"So what do you expect me to do, call a lifeguard?"

"Waiter, there's a dead beetle in my soup!"
"Yes sir. They are not very good swimmers."

"Waiter, there's a fly in my soup!"
"How fortunate, sir. There's usually only enough soup for them to wade."

"Waiter, there's a fly in my soup!"
"You're lucky that it's not HALF a fly!"

"Waiter, there's a fly in my soup!"
"It's possible, sir. The chef used to be a tailor."

Chocolate comes from cocoa, which is a tree, which, in turn, makes it a plant. Therefore, chocolate is salad.
-Sandi Sola

SOUP

"Waiter, there's a fly in my soup!"
"Oh, heavens no, sir. He's not in your soup.
He's been stuck to that bowl for weeks!"

"Waiter, there's a fly in my soup!"
"Don't worry, the tarantula will come up
under him any moment now."

"Waiter, there's a fly in my soup!"
"Yes, sir. He's committed insecticide."

"Waiter, there's a fly in my soup!"
"That can't be, sir. The cook used them all in
the apple pie."

"Waiter, there's a fly in my soup!"
"I'm sorry, sir. That's chicken noodle. You
should have gotten the cockroach with that."

"Waiter, there are two flies in my soup!"
"That's alright, sir. The extra one's on me."

*You know it's time to diet when you push away from
the table and the table moves. -Quoted in* **The Cockle
Bur**

"Waiter, what's this fly doing in my soup?"
"Looks like the backstroke."

"Waiter, there's a dead spider in my soup!"
"Yes, sir. They can't stand the boiling water."

Frog: "Hey Waiter! There's no fly in my soup!"

"Waiter, do you have frogs legs?"
"No, sir. I've always walked like this."

"Waiter, there's a fly in the butter!"
"Yes, sir. It's a butterfly."

"Waiter, how long will my spaghetti be?"
"I don't know. We never measure it."

"Waiter, there's no chicken in this chicken soup!"
"And there's no horse in the horseradish, either."

After years of buying clothes I intend to diet into, I'll say this: the skeleton in my closet has some really nice outfits. -Robert Brault

"Waiter, what's this fly doing on my soup bowl?"
"He's the lifeguard."

SOUP

"Waiter, waiter! I need some coffee without cream."
"I'm sorry, sir, but we're out of cream. Would you like it without milk instead?"

Waiter: "How did you find your steak, sir?"
Customer: "Well, I just pushed aside the peas and there it was!"

"Waiter, there's a fly in my soup!"
"Wait until you see the main course!"

"Waiter, there's a fly in my soup!"
"No, sir. That's a cockroach. The fly is on your steak."

"Waiter, there's a fly in my soup!"
"Oh, did you order a mosquito?"

Diet: a system of starving yourself to death so you can live a little longer. -Totie Fields

"Waiter, there is a small slug in this lettuce."
"I'm sorry, sir. Would you like me to get you a
bigger one?"

"Waiter, there's a beetle in my soup!"
"Sorry, sir. We're out of flies today."

And to a server who just spilled a bowl of
steaming broth in an annoyed customer's lap,
"Waiter, there's a soup in my fly!"

What do you call 2,000 pounds of Chinese
soup?
Won Ton

What are the ingredients of Twitter alphabet
soup?
280 letters

*I go up and down the scale so often that if they ever
perform an autopsy on me they'll find me like a strip of
bacon - a streak of lean and a streak of fat.*
-Texas Guinan

The Main Course
A Smorgasbord of Jokes

Let the derri-aerobics begin!

My wife said she wanted some peace and quiet while she cooked dinner. So I took out the batteries in the smoke alarm.

═══

Q: Why is psychoanalysis a lot quicker for a man than a woman?

A: When it's time to go back to their childhood, they're already there.

═══

I was at the bank the other day. A kind old woman asked me if I wouldn't mind checking her balance. So I pushed her over.

I like rice. Rice is great when you're hungry, and you want 2,000 of something. -Mitch Hedberg

A gorilla at the zoo dies of old age. It is the zoo's most popular attraction by far, so the manager asks one of the employees to wear a gorilla costume and take its place in the cage until they can locate another one. The "human-like" gorilla is extremely popular at first, but the craze wears off after a few weeks. In an attempt to re-invigorate the people's attention, he decides to climb over his enclosure and hang from the net ceiling above the lion's den next to his cage. The people are riveted at this spectacle, but suddenly the man disguised as the gorilla loses his grip and falls to the floor of the lion's den. He begins to scream, "Help! Help!"
The lion pounces on him and whispers in his ear, "Shut up or you're going to get us both fired."

* * *

Cop: Sarge, I'm reporting a strange murder here. A woman shot her husband because he stepped on the floor she just mopped.

Desk Sergeant: Did you arrest her?

Cop: No, not yet. The floor's still wet.

If you stop eating doughnuts you will live three years longer, but it's just three more years that you'll want a doughnut. -Lewis Black

ENTRÉES

Way back when, a caveman was hunting through the jungle when he came upon a huge dead dinosaur with a three-foot pygmy standing beside it. The amazed caveman asked, "Did you kill that?"
"Yep," said the pygmy.
"How could a little guy like you kill that gigantic dinosaur?"
"I did it with my club," the pygmy answered.
"Wow! How big is your club?" asked the caveman.
The pygmy replied, "There are about 70 of us."

===

The school class was looking at the prehistoric animals exhibit while visiting the Museum of Natural History when one of the kids asked the tour guide, "Can you tell me how old those dinosaur bones are?"
The tour guide answered, "They are two million, three years, and two months old."
The teacher of the class was impressed and said, "Wow! How can you be that precise?"
The guide said, "Well, the dinosaur bones were two million years old when I started working here three years and two months ago."

I'm allergic to food. Every time I eat, it breaks out in fat. -Jennifer Greene Duncan

Patient: Doc, I was looking in the mirror and I noticed that one of my eyes is different from the other.

Doctor: Really? Which one?

The job interviewer asks the applicant,
"What do you consider your main strengths and weaknesses?"
The applicant says, "I guess my main weakness would be dealing with reality issues- what's real and what's not."
"And what about your strengths?" asks the interviewer.
"I'm Spider-Man!"

---

19 and 20 had a fight. 21.

Q: What do you get when you cross a bear with a skunk?

A: Winnie the Pew

BrodySwiss cheese is a rip-off. It's the only cheese I can bite into and miss. -Mitch Hedberg

A gorilla was sitting in a tree by the river when a lion came by for a drink. The gorilla thought it'd be a riot to push the king of the jungle in the water, so he swung off the tree and shoved the lion from behind right into the river. The beast came out of the water roaring mad and the gorilla took off running but knew he had to think fast because there was no way he was going to outrun the lion. Just then, he saw a hunter's tent and ducked inside. The hunter was reading a paper at the time but got really frightened and ran out of the tent. The gorilla got a bright idea and pretended to be the hunter. He put on the hunter's shirt and hat and started to make like he was reading the newspaper. A few moments later, the lion ran into the tent and said, "Hey buddy, did you see a gorilla run in here?"

From behind the paper, the disguised gorilla said, "You mean the one that pushed the lion in the river?"

The lion said, "Geeez! It's in the paper already!?"

■ ■ ■

Doctor: I haven't seen you in quite a while.

Patient: I know. I've been ill.

The second day of a diet is always easier than the first. By the second day, you are off it. -Jackie Gleason

Salesman: Ma'am, this super duper vacuum cleaner will cut your work in half.

Woman: Terrific. I'll take two.

···

Patient: Every time I drink a cup of coffee I get a stabbing pain in my right eye. What should I do, Doc?

Doctor: I'd advise you to take the spoon out of your cup.

···

There's a knock on the door of the Pearly Gates. St. Peter answers it and sees a guy there. St. Peter turns around to lead him in to his eternal bliss but the fellow disappears. In a few moments, there's another knock. St. Peter answers it. It's the same guy. And as soon as St. Peter sees him, he vanishes again. A bit later, there's another knock. St. Peter answers it one more time, sees the same guy, and says, "What is this, some kind of game you're playing?" The guy answers, "No, they're trying to resuscitate me."

People on a diet should have a salad dressing called "250 Islands." -George Carlin

The Seafood Plan and Other Fishy Diets

*You know the seafood diet- you see food and you eat it. Here's the skinny on some other weight loss programs, keeping in mind of course, with the Laugh Your A** Off diet, you're losing weight even while reading about them.*

The Garlic Diet: You don't lose weight, you just look thinner from a distance.

The Light Eating Diet: You start eating when it's light out.

The Golfer's Diet: Stay on the greens.

■ ■ ■

"I have a great diet. You're allowed to eat anything you want, but you must eat it with naked fat people." -Ed Bluestone

"There's a great new rice diet that always works - you use one chopstick." -Red Buttons

The only kind of seafood I trust is the fish stick, a totally featureless fish that doesn't have eyeballs or fins. -Dave Barry

ENTRÉES

"My wife is on a diet. Coconuts and bananas. She hasn't lost any weight, but boy can she climb a tree." -Henny Youngman

"Nutri/System…What kind of Nazi diet plan is this? This is where they tell you you have to eat the food they make. They tell you what time of day you have to eat it and you have to eat all of it. This isn't a diet. This is living with your parents." -Destiny

"The cat was not safe when I was on Slimfast. I swear to God. I was chasing the cat. I had soy sauce in one hand, chopsticks in the other. I was like, 'Come here, you little bastard. Mommy's hungry…Oh, I'm sorry, Fluffy. I snapped.'"
-Linda Smith

"I lied on my Weight Watchers list. I put down that I had three eggs… but they were Cadbury chocolate eggs." -Caroline Rhea

Laughing Matters: You want some exercise? Say, "Cheese." Go ahead… There. You just gave your nasolabial folds a workout. They're your "laugh lines," the facial skin folds that run from each side of your nose to the corners of your mouth.

I'm at the age where food has taken the place of sex in my life. In fact, I've just had a mirror put over my kitchen table. -Rodney Dangerfield

A guy visiting his psychiatrist explained that a recent visit with his mother didn't go too well. "What happened?" asked the shrink.
"Well, we were at the dinner table, and I meant to say, 'Pass the salt, please,' but what I said was, 'You witch. You ruined my life!'"

= = =

A masked man stuck a gun into the ribs of a well-dressed man and said, "Give me your money."
The man indignantly responded, "No, I won't. I'm a politician."
The would-be mugger said, "Oh, in that case, give me MY money!"

= = =

A novice hunter came back to the lodge and proudly said, "I shot an elk!"
"How do you know it was an elk?" asked one of the members.
"By his membership card."

My therapist told me the way to achieve true inner peace is to finish what I start. So far today, I have finished two bags of M&M's and a chocolate cake. I feel better already. -Dave Barry

ENTRÉES

Two old golfers were reminiscing as they played. One pointed towards the woods.
"My first girlfriend was named Mary Katherine Agnes Colleen Patricia Marion Margaret Kathleen O'Shaugnessey. Back when I was a lad, working as a caddie, I carved her name in one of those trees right over there."
"What ever happened?" asked his friend.
"The tree fell on me."

###

A husband and wife sat down at a restaurant and noticed there were crumbs all over the table. A waitress came over, wiped down the table and asked them what they wanted.
"I'll just have coffee," said the husband.
"Me too," said the wife, snootily adding, "and make sure the cup is clean."
When the waitress returned with their drinks, she said, "Okay, now which one of you wanted the clean cup?"

###

I had a doctor's appointment but I didn't really want to go, so I called in sick.

Ask not what you can do for your country. Ask what's for lunch. -Orson Welles

ENTRÉES

A male spotted owl was overheard talking to his wife: "What do you mean you have a headache? We're an endangered species!"

...

An FBI agent approached a rancher and said, "We got a tip that you may be growing illegal drugs on your property. Mind if I take a look around?"
The old cowboy replied, "Okay, but don't go over there," as he pointed at one of his fenced-in areas.
The FBI agent pulled out his badge and shoved it into the rancher's face. "I'm a federal agent! I can go wherever I see fit!"
With that, the rancher shrugged and went off to do his daily business. About an hour later he heard a loud scream from the fenced area he had pointed out earlier. He looked and saw the FBI guy sprinting away from a raging bull.
The rancher yelled, "Show him your badge!"

I'm on a bit of a health kick, so I'll take the low-fat vanilla. With the following toppings: Snickles, Gooey Bears, Charlottesville Chew, Nice 'n Many, Kat Kit, Herschel Smooches, Mrs. Badbar, and Milk Dudes.
-Homer Simpson

When I saw my boss in the morning, he told me to have a good day. So I thanked him and went back home.

■ ■ ■

Luigi was about to celebrate his 50th wedding anniversary. His buddy, Mario, asked him the secret to the longevity. "Well, I always tried to treat the wife well," said Luigi, "but actually, the best thing I did was to take her to Italy for our 25th anniversary."
Mario then said, "Wow, how are you going to top that for your 50th?"
"I'm gonna go pick her up."

■ ■ ■

Barney says to Clem, "You wanna hear a really good Batman impersonation?"
Clem says, "Go ahead."
Barney yells, "Oh no, KRYPTONITE!"
Clem says, "That's Superman."
Barney says, "Thanks, Clem. I've been practicing a lot."

I went on a diet. Had to go on two diets at the same time because one wasn't giving me enough food.
-Barry Marder

Q: Why did the guy make it a habit of shaving in front of his car's passenger-side mirror?

A: Because that way he got a closer shave than it actually appears.

···

A guy was shopping for dinner at a supermarket when a beautiful redhead smiled and waved at him. He couldn't figure out where he knew her from but nonetheless he was thrilled at the attention until she walked up and said, "I think you're the father of one of my kids."

Taken aback, he initially denied it but then he searched his memory. "Wait a minute," he blurted out. "That night my buddies got me drunk and took all my clothes and set me out on Main Street and I wandered around until I came into this little bar and fell in the mud-wrestling pit and vomited all over the floor... Were you the stripper who took me home with her that night?"

"No," she answered coolly. "I'm your son's math teacher."

You are what you eat. Which makes me cheap, quick, and easy. -Dave Thomas

ENTRÉES

Q: Why did the rubber chicken cross the road?

A: To stretch its legs

■ ■ ■

A disconsolate man takes his goldfish to the vet
and says, "Doc, I think it has epilepsy."
The vet takes a look and replies, "Gee, it seems
calm enough to me."
The man says, "Wait until you see what happens
when I take it out of the bowl."

■ ■ ■

Harold walks into a library and announces, "I'll
have steak."
The librarian says, "This is a library, sir."
Harold whispers, "Oh, I'm sorry. I'll have steak."

■ ■ ■

Q: How come the invisible man decided not to
have children?

A: He didn't want to become apparent.

My life today is tough. My wife, she's attached to a
machine that keeps her alive - the refrigerator.
-Rodney Dangerfield

Melvin: My pet hamster died.

Roger: Sorry to hear that. What happened?

Melvin: He fell asleep at the wheel.

■ ■ ■

What do you get when you cross a joke with a rhetorical question?

■ ■ ■

Two psychics run into each other on a terribly frigid day. One says to the other, "It's an awfully cold winter we're having, isn't it?"
"Yes," responds the other. "It reminds me of the winter of 2046."

■ ■ ■

Q: What did one fly say to the other fly?

A: Hey, fly, your dude is open.

■ ■ ■

Two ducks were in a pond. One went, "Quack quack!" and the other duck said, "That's funny, I was just about to say that!"

Health food makes me sick. -Calvin Trillin

E
N
T
R
Ê
E
S

Bertha: Doc, you gotta do something about my husband. He thinks he's a refrigerator.

Shrink: I wouldn't worry about it if I were you. Lots of people have harmless temporary delusions. He'll probably get over it.

Bertha: Maybe you wouldn't worry about it, but I can't take it. He sleeps with his mouth open and the little light keeps me awake.

■■■

A doctor examines a woman, then goes into the waiting room and says to the husband, "I don't want to scare you, but I don't like the way your wife looks."

The husband says, "Me neither, but she's a wonderful cook and is good with the kids."

■■■

A bank robber points a gun at the teller and says, "Give me all the money or you're geography!"
The teller responds, "Didn't you mean to say 'or you're history'?"
The robber says, "Don't change the subject!"

Diets are for those who are thick and tired of it.
-Mary Tyler Moore

Good News/Bad News

An artist asked the gallery owner if there had been any interest in his paintings.

"Good news and bad news," said the owner. "A fellow asked about your work and wondered if it would appreciate in value after your death. When I assured him that it would, he bought all twelve of your paintings."

"Wonderful," said the artist. "What could the bad news possibly be?"

"He was your doctor."

●●●

The doctor says to his patient, "I've got some good news and some bad news about your upcoming surgery."

The patient says, "Give me the bad news first."

"It's an extremely risky procedure and chances of survival are only 99 to one."

"That's horrible," says the patient. "What could the good news possibly be?"

"My last 99 patients died."

I've been on a constant diet for the last two decades. I've lost a total of 789 pounds. By all accounts, I should be hanging from a charm bracelet. -Erma Bombeck

Wife: Honey, I've got some good news and bad news about the car.

Hubbie: Gimme the good news first.

Wife: The air bag works.

■ ■ ■

A lawyer, meeting with his client in prison, says, "I've got some good news and bad news."
The client says, "Give me the bad news first."
"Your DNA matches the blood found on the victim as well as the murder weapon."
"What could the good news possibly be?" asks the client.
"Your cholesterol is down to 120."

■ ■ ■

One day a guy made an airplane jump. There was some good news and some bad news.
Good News: He had a parachute.
Bad News: It didn't open.
Good News: There was a haystack down below.
Bad News: There was a pitchfork in the haystack.
Good News: He missed the pitchfork.
Bad News: He missed the haystack.

Health nuts are going to feel stupid someday, lying in hospitals dying of nothing. -Redd Foxx

Doctor, in the delivery room: I have some bad news and some worse news.

Patient, after giving birth: Okay, well... give me the bad news first.

Doctor: You gave birth to an eight pound eyeball.

Patient: An eyeball!? What could be worse?

Doctor: It's blind.

Laughing Matters: No one actually knows for sure, but it's been widely circulated that it takes 17 muscles to smile, 43 to frown.

Bertha asked her husband for the newspaper. He replied, "Newspaper? My dear, we're living in a digital world and you're still asking for the newspaper? Here, take my iPad instead."
So she took the iPad and killed the cockroach.

...

Chester: A man knocked on my door today and asked for a small donation for the local swimming pool.

Lester: What did you give him?

Chester: A glass of water.

I'm trying to lose 25 lbs. - Only 30 to go! -Jack Kreismer

ENTRÉES

The veteran village blacksmith hired a new young apprentice eager to work 24/7. Teaching the boy, the blacksmith said, "When I take the shoe out of the fire, I will lay it on the anvil. When I nod my head, you strike it with the hammer."
The apprentice did precisely what he was told and he's now the new village blacksmith.

===

Ralph is new to the apartment complex and says to his neighbor, "Wally, you've got the same studio apartment as mine. How many rolls of wallpaper did you use to paper it?"
"I bought eight rolls," replies Wally.
A few weeks later Ralph says, "Hey, Wally. I wallpapered my apartment and had four rolls left over."
Wally says, "Yeah, so did I."

===

"If we get engaged, will you give me a ring?" the girl asks her lover.
"Sure. What's your phone number?"

People say that losing weight is no walk in the park. When I hear that, I think, "Yeah, that's the problem."
-Chris Adams

What do you call a guy buried in a garden?
Pete

What do you call a guy under a car?
Jack

What do you call a guy in a catapult?
Chuck

What do you call a guy in a pile of leaves?
Russell

What do you call an Italian guy with a rubber
toe?
Roberto

What do you call a guy with a shovel stuck in his
head?
Doug

What do you call a guy WITHOUT a shovel stuck
in his head?
Douglas

What do you call a French guy in sandals?
Philippe Philoppe

*I don't stop eating when I'm full. The meal isn't over
when I'm full. It's over when I hate myself. -Louis C.K.*

ENTRÉES

A pair of elderly couples were chatting at dinner when one of the husbands said, "Bentley, how was that memory clinic you went to last week?"
"Great," answered Bentley. "We were taught all the latest and greatest memory helpers - association, visualization - that kind of stuff."
"Sounds good... I might like to take a class. What was the name of it?"
Bentley's mind went blank. Then he suddenly smiled and said, "What do you call that flower that's red with a long stem and thorns?"
His buddy said, "You mean a rose?"
Bentley said, "Yeah, that's it," then turned to his wife and asked, "What was the name of that memory clinic, Rose?"

A priest and a minister are holding up a sign alongside the road. It reads, "The end is near! Turn around before it is too late!"
A driver shouts, "Get out of my way," speeds on past and then, from around the bend, the clergymen hear screeching tires followed by a big splash.
The priest says to the minister, "Do you think maybe we should have just put up a sign that says 'Bridge Out'?"

I think I just ate my willpower. -Nancy O'Brien

ENTRÉES

A guy had been stranded on an island for ages. One day as he was walking on the beach, a beautiful woman in a wetsuit emerged from the surf. "Hey, cutie pie. Have you been here long?" she asked.

"I reckon about ten years."

"Do you smoke?"

"Oh, what I'd do for a cigarette!" he moaned. With that, she unzipped a pocket in the sleeve of her wetsuit, pulled out a pack of cigarettes, lit one and gave it to him.

"I guess it's been a long while since you've had a drink, huh?"

"You got that right," he said.

She pulled out a flask from another pocket, gave it to him and he anxiously took a long, hard swig.

"I bet you haven't played around in a while either," she cooed as she began to unzip the front of her wetsuit.

Positively wide-eyed with anticipation, he gasped, "Don't tell me you have a set of golf clubs in there too?!"

Let's face it, Americans are fat all year round, but the holidays are when we really hit our stride. And you can bet the food we eat will be just as unhealthy as the families we're forced to visit. -Lewis Black

Norman was walking his dog when the seductive aroma of an Italian restaurant he was passing called him to lunch. He decided to take his Chihuahua into the restaurant with him, so he donned dark glasses and tapped his way into the establishment. After seeing the man, a waiter remarked, "Hey Mister- you can't bring a dog in here."

Norman indignantly replied, "I'm blind and this is my Seeing Eye dog."

"You trying to tell me this Chihuahua is a Seeing Eye dog?" the waiter demanded.

"What?" cried Norman. "They gave me a Chihuahua?"

···

An 8-year-old girl asked, "Daddy, what is sex?" The surprised father was taken aback but decided that if she was old enough to ask the question, she was old enough to get an answer. After telling her all about the birds and the bees, he said, "Why do you ask?"

Still a little wide-eyed, the little girl replied, "Mom told me to tell you that dinner would be ready in just a couple of secs."

Health Food: any food whose flavor is indistinguishable from that of the package in which it is sold. -Henry Beard

Fat Chants

"Is she fat? Her favorite food is seconds."
-Joan Rivers

"When you have a fat friend there are no seesaws. Only catapults." -Demetri Martin

"I'm not overweight. I'm just nine inches too short." -Shelley Winters

"You know you're getting fat when you sit in your bathtub and the water in the toilet rises."
-Etta May

"It's okay to be fat. So you're fat. Just be fat and shut up about it." -Roseanne Barr

"This girl was fat. I hit her with my car. She asked me, 'Why didn't you go around me?' I told her, 'I didn't have enough gas.'"
-Rodney Dangerfield

"We're all concerned about your weight. Bart said NASA called. They said that your gravity is pulling all the satellites out of orbit."
-Marge Simpson, to Homer

No man is lonely while eating spaghetti. -Robert Morley

ENTRÉES

"You're getting so big I need double vision to take you in." -Peter De Vries

"You know you're getting fat when you can pinch an inch on your forehead."
-John Mendoza

"I won't tell you how much I weigh, but don't ever get on an elevator with me unless you're going down." -Jack E. Leonard

Anonymous Musings:

You're not fat. You're just easier to see.

Obesity is a condition which proves that the Lord does not help those who help themselves and help themselves and help themselves.

250 lbs on Earth is only 94 lbs on Mars. I'm not fat. I'm just on the wrong planet.

9 out of 10 voices in my head are telling me that I am too fat. The last one is calmly preparing a bowl of chips.

If I cut mysef shaving, sausage gravy comes out. That's why I keep a pile of biscuits next to the sink. -Drew Carey

I think I need to lose some weight. I tried to sit up earlier and ended up rocking myself to sleep.

Don't pick on fat people. They have enough on their plates.

I am in shape. Round is a shape.

When things heat, they expand… I'm not fat, I'm HOT!

Laughing Matters: An average person laughs approximately 13 times a day.

One evening, a policeman was staking out a tavern for possible driving-under-the-influence variations. When the bar closed, he saw a fellow come stumbling out, stagger to his car and fumble with his keys before he got into the driver's seat. Finally, he started the engine and took off, only to find the cop waiting for him. The officer approached the driver, read him his rights and gave the guy a breathalyzer test. The results showed a reading of 0.0. The cop demanded to know how that could be.

The guy responded, "Tonight, I'm the designated decoy."

I eat merely to put food out of my mind. -N.F. Simpson

ENTRÊES

A woman heading to work walked by a pet shop with a parrot sitting out front on a perch. The parrot squawked, "Hey, ugly lady! Hey, ugly lady!"

The woman was furious. When she came home that evening and strolled by the pet shop, the parrot repeated, "Hey, ugly lady! Hey, ugly lady!"

She stormed into the pet shop and told the owner in no uncertain terms of her displeasure with the parrot's outbursts. The owner promised her it wouldn't happen again. The next day, as she passed by the pet shop, there was the parrot out front again. The bird squawked, "Hey!"

The woman turned to parrot and said, "Hey, what?"

The parrot said, "You know…"

...

Two runners were trailing the pack in the marathon. The guy who was second-to-last was poking fun at the runner behind him.

"Hey, how does it feel to be last?"

"Well, if you must know," said the other guy… And then he dropped out.

I'm trying to get back to my original weight- eight pounds, three ounces. -Cheril Vendetti

Two cannibals went to their favorite restaurant. "Look," said one, "there's a politician on the menu tonight."
"Sweet," said the other. "I love baloney sandwiches."

* * *

"Do you know about the birds and the bees?" asks Little Johnny's father.
"I don't want to know!" Little Johnny says, bursting into tears.
Johnny's father is perplexed and asks him what's wrong.
Little Johnny sobs, "First, there was no Santa Claus, then no Easter Bunny, and then no Tooth Fairy. If you're gonna tell me that grownups don't really have sex, I've got nothing left to believe in."

* * *

The sergeant scolded the private, "You failed to show up for camouflage class yesterday!"
The private responded, "And how do you know that, Sarge?"

If you really want to be depressed, weigh yourself in grams. -Jason Love

ENTRÉES

Two guys are out hunting when they come across some tracks in the woods. The first guy says, "Look, moose tracks."
The second one says, "No. Those are deer tracks. I know deer tracks when I see 'em."
A few moments later, they both got run over by a train.

░░░

A fighter was in the ring with Siamese twins. After the bout he returned home and his wife asked, "Did you win?"
He answered, "Yes and no."

░░░

Sam and Moe were rocking on the porch at the retirement home.
Having talked about everything under the sun, Sam was grasping for a new topic of conversation. "Tell me, Moe, have you read Marx?" Sam asked.
"Yes," replied Moe. "And, you know, I think it's the wicker chairs."

I swallowed a tape worm last night. It's going to grow up to three feet inside of me, and then it eats all of my food so that I don't get fat. -Kelly Kapoor, TV's The Office

ENTRÉES

A guy sits down at the bar and the bartender asks, "What'll it be?"
The guy says, "I'll have a scotch, please."
The bartender gives him the drink, and says, "That'll be eight dollars."
The guy responds, "What do you mean? I don't owe you anything for this."
A lawyer who was sitting nearby and overheard the conversation comments to the bartender, "You know, actually he's right. In the initial offer, which constitutes a binding contract upon acceptance, there was no stipulation of remuneration of any kind."
The bartender is clearly not impressed, but nonetheless, turns to the guy and says, "Okay, Bud, you beat me for a drink. But don't ever come in here again."
The next day, the same guy walks into the bar. The bartender yells, "What are you doing in here? I told you never to come back!"
The guy says, "What are you talking about? I've never been in this bar in my life!"
The bartender replies, "I'm very sorry, sir, but this is remarkable. You must have a double."
The guy says, "Thanks. Make it a scotch."

I eat when I'm depressed and I eat when I'm happy. When I can't decide whether I'm tired or hungry, I make the decision while I'm eating. -Oprah Winfrey

A priest went to buy a parrot. The pet shop owner said, "Father, I have just the bird for you. It doesn't scream, yell or swear. In fact, it's a religious parrot. You see those strings on his legs? When you pull the left one, he recites the Lord's Prayer. When you pull the right one, he recites the 23rd Psalm."

"Terrific," exclaimed the priest. "And what happens if you pull both strings?"

The parrot squawked, "I fall off my perch, you idiot!"

...

Little Johnny's mother, in an attempt to get him to stop sucking his thumb, told him that if he continued to do so his stomach would get bigger and bigger until it burst.

Later that day, they went to the supermarket, where Johnny saw a very pregnant woman. Noticing that he was staring at her, the woman said, "You don't know me. You shouldn't be staring at me."

Johnny replied, "I may not know you, but I know what you've been doing!"

I'm tired of all this nonsense about beauty being only skin-deep. That's deep enough. What do you want, an adorable pancreas? -Rita Mae Brown

An inquisitive baby camel asks her mom, "Why do we have big, three-toed feet?"

Momma camel responds, "Well, son, when we travel across the desert, your toes will help to keep you on top of the soft sand."

"Okay, Mom," says the baby camel, "And why do I have these really long eyelashes?"

"That's to keep the sand out of your eyes when we're in the desert."

The baby camel thinks for a few moments and then asks, "Why do I have these great big humps on my back?"

Momma camel is getting a little impatient with her son's questions, but answers, "They are for storing water for our long treks across the desert."

"I see," says the baby camel, "So we have big feet to keep us from sinking in the sand, long eyelashes to keep the sand out of our eyes, and we have humps to store water, but Mom…"

"What now?" interrupts the exasperated Momma camel.

"Why are we in the San Diego Zoo?"

My favorite health club is the International House of Pancakes. Because no matter what you weigh, there will always be someone who weighs 150 pounds more than you. -Lewis Black

ENTRÉES

A guy is standing on the curb, about to cross the road. As soon as he steps down onto the street, a car heads straight at him. He moves faster, but so does the vehicle. The guy thinks better of going across the street and moves quickly back, but the car changes lanes and is heading right for him. The guy freezes right in the middle of the road and the car comes screeching to a halt. The driver rolls down the window. Behind the wheel is a squirrel. "See," the squirrel says, "It's not as easy as it looks, is it?"

- - -

Teacher: Johnny, use the word "discount" in a sentence.

Johnny: Okay… Does discount as a sentence?

- - -

"Hey, Grandpa, can you make a noise like a frog?" asked Little Johnny.
"Why do you want me to do that, Johnny?"
"Because Mom said when you croak, we're goin' to Disney World!"

The biggest seller is cookbooks and the second is diet books - how not to eat what you've just learned how to cook. -Andy Rooney

Food For Thought

ENTRÉES

A panhandler approached a well-dressed woman who was shopping on Fifth Avenue and said, "I haven't eaten anything in six days." She responded, "God, I wish I had your willpower."

...

What do clocks eat?

Mostly hours-d'oeuvres, in minute amounts, but they usually take seconds.

...

A woman is standing before the judge in a packed courtroom. The judge asks, "What is it that you stole from the grocery store, ma'am?" "Only a small can of a half dozen peaches," pleaded the woman. "That'll be six nights in jail- one night for each stolen peach," declares the judge. The woman is crestfallen. She looks like she's just about to faint when her husband hollers from the back of the courtroom, "She stole a can of peas, too!"

I am not a vegetarian because I love animals; I am a vegetarian because I hate plants. -A. Whitney Brown

A dietician is conducting a seminar before a huge crowd. He tells the folks, "Much of the food we eat today is extremely unhealthful. Red meat is dangerous. Many vegetables are sprayed with pesticides and are unsafe. Drinking water can be contaminated. However, there is one food that is far and away the most dangerous of all. Can anyone tell me what it is?"

Following a long pause, a man in the back sticks his hand up and yells, "Wedding cake!"

= = =

A New Yorker calls his mother who lives in Florida. She answers the phone with a very weak-sounding voice.

"Mom, you don't sound good. What's wrong?"

Very feebly she answers, "I haven't eaten in quite some time."

"How long has it been, Mom?"

"My last meal was 26 days ago."

"26 days! How come?"

"I didn't want to be caught with food in my mouth when you called."

I went to this restaurant last night that was set up like a big buffet in the shape of a Ouija board. You'd think about what kind of food you want, and the table would move across the floor to it. -Steven Wright

ENTRÉES

A husband is on his way out to the store when the wife says, "Please pick up a carton of milk and if they have eggs, get me a dozen."
The husband returns home with 12 cartons of milk.
"Why on earth would you get me 12 cartons of milk?" asks the wife.
"They had eggs."

■ ■ ■

While doing research on a South Pacific Island, a scientist discovered a rare bird in the jungle that, through years of contact with missionaries, had learned to speak ten different languages. He was amazed and shipped the prized bird home to his wife in a special cage as a surprise anniversary gift.
A month later he arrived home from his expedition. His wife welcomed him with the news that in celebration of his arrival, she had cooked the bird as the main course in his welcome home dinner.
"You cooked the bird I sent home from the South Pacific!?" the man shouted. "It spoke ten languages!"
"Ten languages?" replied his surprised wife. "He should have said something."

Never eat more than you can lift. -Miss Piggy

A guy goes into a seafood store with a salmon under his arm. He asks the owner, "Do you make fish cakes here?"

"Sure," says the fishmonger.

"Good. It's his birthday."

• • •

A rabbit hopped into a butcher shop and asked, "Do you have any carrots?"

"No," said the butcher.

The next day the rabbit showed up and said, "Have any carrots?"

"If I told you once, I told you twice- The answer is NO," said the butcher.

The following day the rabbit appeared again and said, "Got any carrots?"

The butcher angrily replied, "N-O, NO! And if you come back in here again and ask for carrots, I'll hammer you to the wall by your ears!"

The next day the rabbit came back and asked, "Do you have any nails?"

"No," said the butcher.

"Good ... Do you have any carrots?"

Laughing Matters: Laughter really may be the best medicine. A Norwegian study of over 50,000 people found that a strong sense of humor may extend life expectancy.

Avoid any diet that discourages the use of hot fudge.
-Don Kardong

Once upon a time an evil witch placed a spell over a prince, whereby he could speak only one word a year. He was permitted, though, to save up words. If he didn't speak a word in a given year, for example, he would be allowed two words the next year.

One day the prince encountered an absolutely stunning princess and fell head over heels for her. He decided not to speak for two years so that he could look at her and say, "My sweetheart." At the end of the two years, however, he wanted to tell her that he also loved her, so he decided to wait three more years- making for a total of five years of silence. Then, after five years, he knew he wanted to ask her to marry him, so he needed to wait four more years to speak- nine years in all. Finally, at the end of that period, the prince would be able to speak his piece.

With great anticipation, he led the princess into the royal garden where he knelt before her.

He spoke those nine precious words that he'd waited nine long years to be able to deliver.

"My sweetheart, I love you. Will you marry me?" She replied, "Pardon?"

When the waitress asked if I wanted my pizza cut into four or eight slices, I said, "Four. I don't think I can eat eight." -Yogi Berra

ENTRÉES

"How can I help you, Harold?" asked the pastor.
"I need you to pray for my hearing," said the
obviously distraught church member.
With that, the pastor cupped his hands around
Harold's ears and prayed. When he finished he
said, "How is your hearing now, Harold?"
"I don't know," Harold replied. "The hearing
isn't until next Monday."

...

Three old geezers were sitting on a bench in
New York City's Central Park. The one in the
middle was reading a newspaper while the other
two were pretending to fish. A policeman on
the beat watched them as they baited imaginary
hooks, cast their lines and reeled in their fake
catches.
"Do you know these two?" the cop asked the
guy reading the paper.
"Sure. They're buddies of mine."
"Well, they're disturbin' the other people. You
better get them outta here!"
"Yes, officer," said the guy. With that, he
furiously began rowing.

*What's the two things they tell you are healthiest to
eat? Chicken and fish. You know what you should do?
Combine them, eat a penguin. -Dave Attell*

ENTRÉES

Exorcise Exercise!

"The word aerobics came about when the gym instructors got together and said, 'If we're going to charge $10 an hour, we can't call it jumping up and down.'" -Rita Rudner

"I joined a health club last year, spent 400 bucks. Haven't lost a pound. Apparently you have to show up." -Rich Ceisler

"I believe that the Good Lord gave us a finite number of heartbeats and I'm damned if I'm going to use up mine running up and down a street." -Neil Armstrong, on jogging

"I struggle with laziness. I'm like, 'Should I sit down and do nothing or lie down and do nothing?'" -Jim Gaffigan

"My grandmother began walking five miles a day when she was 82. Now we don't know where the hell she is." -Ellen DeGeneres

"I bought an exercise bicycle two years ago... the most expensive coat hanger in New York." -Robert Klein

I'm so compulsive about weight, I weigh myself after I cough. -Elayne Boosler

"The only exercise program that has ever worked for me is occasionally getting up in the morning and jogging my memory to remind myself exactly how much I hate to exercise."
-Dennis Miller

"A friend of mine runs marathons. He always talks about this 'runner's high.' But he has to go 26 miles for it. That's why I smoke and drink. I get the same feeling from a flight of stairs."
-Larry Miller

"My idea of exercise is a good brisk sit." -Phyllis Diller

"I consider exercise vulgar. It makes people smell." -Alec Yuill-Thornton

"I live alone. I'm not married. I hope to be someday so I can stop exercising." -Jeff Stilson

"My exercise routine consists of doing diddly squats." -Andrew Greenwood

"I don't exercise. If God had wanted me to bend over, he would have put diamonds on the floor."
-Joan Rivers

Observe your dog: if he's fat, then you're not getting enough exercise. -Evan Esar

Anonymous Musings:

Does running late count as exercise?

I call my bathroom "Jim" so I can say I go to the "Jim" every morning.

I took to heart my doctor's advice to get more exercise. Just one problem- I thought he said, "EXTRA FRIES!"

Wouldn't exercise be more fun if calories screamed while you burned them?

I am known at the gym as the "before picture."

I'm gonna go for a walk because I want to stay healthy. I'm taking along a Snickers bar because let's be honest here.

Do people who go to the gym to "feel the burn" know nothing of Mexican food?

I consider my refusal to go to the gym today as resistance training.

I really don't think I need buns of steel. I'd be happy with buns of cinnamon. -Ellen DeGeneres

ENTRÉES

I signed up for an exercise class and was told to wear loose-fitting clothing. If I had any loose-fitting clothing, I wouldn't have signed up in the first place.

I'm not into working out. My philosophy: No pain, no pain.

I don't exercise at all. If God meant for us to touch our toes, he would have put them further up our body.

I entered everything I ate today into my new fitness app and it just sent an ambulance to my house.

Laughing Matters: Loma Linda University researchers discovered that laughter improved the memory of senior citizens.

Donald Trump visits an old folks' home to mingle with the people and pick up some good P.R. at the same time. He walks up to a sweet old lady in a wheelchair who smiles at him with an otherwise blank stare.
"Do you know who I am?" he says.
She responds, "No, but if you ask at the desk, they'll tell you."

I've been on a diet for two weeks and all I've lost is fourteen days. -Totie Fields

A woman says to her physician, "Doctor you have to help me- I think I'm addicted to Twitter."
"Sorry," the doctor replied. "I don't follow you."

■■■

The traffic was backed up even more than usual and people were getting out of their cars to find out what was up. Herbie strolled up to the driver ahead of him and asked what was going on.
"Apparently, some nut hijacked a busload of lawyers and is holding them for ransom. He says he wants $10,000 or he'll douse the bus with gasoline and set it on fire. These guys with the buckets are taking up a collection."
"Oh really?" Herbie said with concern. "How much is everyone giving?"
The driver replied, "About a gallon."

■■■

A millipede bumps into a centipede on the street. "What are the odds of this?" says the surprised millipede.
The centipede answers, "About 10 to 1."

I tried every diet in the book. I tried some that weren't in the book. I tried eating the book. It tasted better than most of the diets. -Dolly Parton

Polly: I had a double-whammy of a bad day.

Molly: What happened?

Polly: My ex got run over by a bus.

Molly: Wow! What else happened?

Polly: I got fired from my bus driving job.

Maxy Segal, serving 10 years in the pen, got a letter from his wife: "Dear Maxy, I wanted to grow some lettuce but since you're the one with the green thumb, I wondered when would be the best time to plant it in the garden."
Knowing that the guards read all the prisoner's mail, he replied: "My Dear Wife, Whatever you do, don't dig up the garden. I buried the loot from the heist there!"
About a week later, Maxy received another letter from his better half: "Dear Maxy, I don't know what happened. A few days ago, fifty men with shovels showed up and dug up the entire garden."
Maxy sent his reply immediately: "My Dear Wife, It is now time to plant."

The first thing you lose on a diet is brain mass.
-Margaret Cho

Two cowboys are riding along out West when they hear the ominous sound of drums. One of the cowboys says, "I don't like the sound of those drums."
Off in the distance, they hear an Indian yell, "He's not our regular drummer!"

•••

A psychiatrist came home from a convention in Utah, where the delegates spent more time on the ski slopes than in the conference rooms. His wife asked him, "So, how did it go?"
"Pretty good," he answered, "but I've never seen so many Freudians slip."

•••

A woman visits an art gallery and sees two very similar still-life paintings, both of a table spread out for lunch and both portraying a glass of wine, a basket of bread rolls and a plate of sliced ham. One painting, however, is selling for $100 and the other for $75. The woman is curious about the price differential and asks the gallery owner about it. The owner responds, "You get more ham with the $100 painting."

I never worry about diets. The only carrots that interest me are the number you get in a diamond. -Mae West

ENTRÉES

A man and his wife were out for a drive when a cop pulled them over. As the officer approached the car, the man rolled down his window. The cop said, "Excuse me, sir. Were you aware that you were driving well over the speed limit?" The driver responded, "Why, no officer, I wasn't aware of that."

With that, his wife exclaimed, "Who are you kidding? You were going at least 20 miles over the limit!"

The cop then asked, "And I noticed you weren't wearing a seat belt. How come?"

He answered, "Well, officer, when I saw you approach the car I figured I'd probably have to get out so I took it off."

His wife then said, "What are you talking about? You never wear a seat belt."

At that point, the cop leaned in and said to the wife, "Does your husband always lie like this?"

"Oh, not always, officer," she replied sweetly. "Only when he's had way too much to drink."

Celery has negative calories. It takes more energy to chew it than the food contains. I was thinking about this: If you eat 30 pounds of celery for seven days, you could disappear. The seventh day you are kind of chomping away, getting kind of transparent, getting a green hue, kind of going...Poof! -Tim Bedore

Weighing In

Gertrude: I'm getting so upset over arguing with my husband all the time. With all the stress, I've lost 15 pounds.

Mabel: Maybe you should consider splitting up.

Gertrude: Not yet. I'd like to lose another 10 pounds.

= = =

Ralph forgot his wedding anniversary and his wife was more than a bit agitated. "Tomorrow morning, I expect to find a gift in the driveway that goes from 0 to 200 in five seconds. And it better be there or else!" she yelled.
The next morning, she got up, looked out the window and, sure enough, there was a gift-wrapped box, smack in the middle of the driveway. The wife put on her robe and slippers, ran outside and opened it up right then and there- a bathroom scale.

= = =

He was so fat, to get all of him in the picture, they had to use Google Earth.

Dieting is when you eat food that makes you sad.
-Lori Bealler

He was so fat, his stretch limo had to stretch sideways.

...

A tipsy guy walks up to a parking meter. He puts in a quarter, the needle stops at 60 and he exclaims, "I can't believe I lost 100 pounds!"

...

A woman is watching her husband suck in his gut as he's standing on the bathroom scale. "Ha, that's not going to help," she chides him. "Sure is," answers her hubby. "It's the only way I can see the numbers."

...

Wally: Wow you look great! Did you lose weight?

Molly: Hey- did you just call me ugly and fat in retrospect?!

...

How much does a hipster weigh?
An Instagram

I would lose weight, but I hate losing. -Jim Tomlinson

I stepped on the scale and it said, "I need your weight, not your phone number."

I stepped on the scale and it said, "One at a time, please."

I stepped on the scale and it said, "To be continued."

Laughing Matters: CNN reports that, not only is laughter the most effortless way to burn calories, it releases serotonin, a feel-good hormone that has properties which can curb your appetite.

A waiter dies suddenly and his widow is so distraught that she seeks out a medium who assures her that she can speak to her husband. At the appointed time, the widow goes to a séance, presses her hands on the table and calls out, "Seymour, Seymour, oh how I miss you! Please, please speak to me!"
There's a terrible shriek and scary noises followed by a faint voice which cries out, "Sorry, it's not my table!"

I told my doctor I get very tired when I go on a diet, so he gave me pep pills. Know what happened? I ate faster. -Joe E. Lewis

ENTRÉES

Two women are having conversation about their psychotherapists. One says, "My shrink drives me crazy. She answers every question with a question. Sometimes I think I'm just throwing good money after bad."
The other woman says, "I should be so lucky. I've been paying mine $300 a session for three years and he hadn't said one single word until yesterday."
"Really? What did he say?"
"No hablo Ingles."

Bill Gates appeared at the Pearly Gates where St. Peter said, "Allow me to escort you to your heavenly home." With that, Gates was brought to a little bungalow in the woods.
Right next door was a huge estate, complete with an Olympic size swimming pool, tennis court and a golf course. "My gosh. Who lives there?" Gates asked St. Peter.
"The captain of the Titanic," answered St. Peter.
"How come he gets a better eternal home than me?" asked Gates.
St. Peter replied, "Because the Titanic only crashed once."

The best ab exercise is 3 sets of stop eating so much crap. -Mike Sauter

At the Summer Olympic Games, a girl bumped into a guy carrying an eight-foot long stick. "Excuse me," said the girl, "but are you by any chance a pole vaulter?"
"Nein, I'm a German, but how did you know my name is Valter?"

= = =

A husband and wife, both golf fanatics, were discussing the future as they sat by a warm fireplace. "Dear," the wife said, "if I died, would you remarry?"
The husband responded, "Well, if something were to happen to you in the near future, I guess so. After all, we're not exactly senior citizens."
"Would you live in this house with her?" the wife asked.
"I would think so."
She continued, "How about my car? Would she get that?"
"I don't see why not."
"What about my golf clubs? Would you give them to her too?"
"Not a chance in the world!" the husband exclaimed. "She's left-handed."

I just burned 1200 calories. I left the pizza in the oven.
-Maxine Tauber

ENTRÉES

Q: What did the schizophrenic bookkeeper say?

A: I hear invoices!

                     * * *

A guy walks into a lawyer's office and asks,
"What are your rates?"
"Two hundred dollars for three questions,"
answers the lawyer.
"That's a pretty hefty charge, isn't it?"
"Maybe," the lawyer responds. "What's your
final question?"

                     * * *

Herbie was sent to prison. In time, the warden
made arrangements for him to learn a trade
and so Herbie became a carpenter. In fact, he
became so good that once he got out of the
slammer, he was known as one of the best in the
business in his town.
When the warden needed some remodeling
done, he called Herbie in and asked if he'd build
some cabinets and countertops in his kitchen.
Herbie said to the warden, "I wish I could help
you, but I'm afraid I can't. Counterfitting is what
got me into jail in the first place."

McDonald's double cheeseburgers are a weapon of
mass destruction. -Ralph Nader

A family of three country bumpkins were visiting the Empire State Building in New York. The mother paused to view the magnificent art in the lobby. The father and son went on ahead and, for the first time in their lives, saw an elevator. They were perplexed by the sliding doors and couldn't imagine what the little room was for. Just then, an elderly woman walked up and hit the button. The doors opened and she stepped in. The boy and his dad watched as the doors closed. Moments later, a little bell sounded, the doors opened and out stepped a voluptuous 18-year-old beauty that any country boy would be proud to have as a kissin' cousin. The father was simply amazed and, keeping his eye on the elevator, tapped the boy on the shoulder. "Billy-Bob," he said intently, "go get your mother."

* * *

A guy walks into a crowded room and shouts, "All lawyers are idiots!"
A fellow in the back of the room yells, "I resent that remark."
The guy says, "Why? Are you a lawyer?"
"No, I'm an idiot."

I won't be impressed with technology until I can download food. -Bill Pereira

ENTRÉES

Q: Why did the chicken cross the road?

A: Because she heard that on the other side of the road there was a construction guy laying bricks and thought to herself, "This I gotta see."

＝＝＝

A savvy antique collector is strolling in the city when he sees an old cat lapping milk from an old saucer outside a thrift shop. He detects that the saucer is very valuable. He goes into the shop and says to the owner that he'd like to buy the cat. "I'll give you twenty dollars."
"Sorry, but the cat's not for sale," says the owner.
"Tell you what," says the antique collector. "I really need a cat around the house to catch mice. I'll give you fifty bucks."
"Deal," says the owner, and he hands over the cat.
Then the antique collector slyly suggests, "Hey, could you throw in the old saucer for an extra couple of bucks? The cat's used to it and I won't have to go looking for a dish."
The thrift shop owner says, "Sorry, bud, but that's my lucky saucer. So far this week I've sold 28 cats."

I am not a glutton - I am an explorer of food.
-Erma Bombeck

Husband: Doc! My wife's in labor, but keeps screaming, "Shouldn't, couldn't, wouldn't!"

Doctor: Not to worry. She's just having contractions.

...

There was an old Frenchman who got up at the crack of dawn every morning and would go out and sprinkle the local roads with white powder. When a cop asked him what he was sprinkling, he claimed it was elephant powder. The cop scoffed, "But there are no elephants in France!" The old geezer replied, "See- it works!"

...

Horace applied for a job in the supermarket and volunteered that he had experience, having previously worked in another grocery store. When the interviewer asked why he had left, Horace said, "I was fired for spending too much time with the meat slicer."
The interviewer was baffled and said, "That doesn't sound like a serious offense to me."
"Well, they must have thought so," replied Horace. "They fired her, too."

My advice if you insist on slimming: Eat as much as you like - just don't swallow it. -Harry Secombe

Two dogs were standing by a parking meter when one said to the other, "How do you like that? Pay toilets!"

■ ■ ■

A woman got on a bus holding a baby. The bus driver said, "That's the ugliest baby I've ever seen."
In a huff, the woman slammed her fare into the fare box and took an aisle seat near the rear of the bus. The man next to her saw that she was agitated and asked her what was wrong. "The bus driver insulted me," she fumed.
The guy said, "He's a public servant and shouldn't say things to insult passengers."
"You're right," she said. "I think I'll go back up there and give him a piece of my mind."
"Good idea," the man said. "Here, let me hold your monkey."

■ ■ ■

Patient: Doc, I slipped in the grocery story and got injured badly.

Doctor: Where did you get hurt?

Patient: Aisle four.

I will not eat oysters. I want my food dead. Not sick. Not wounded. Dead. -Woody Allen

Q: Why did the Pope cross the road?

A: He crosses everything.

...

A Boston marathoner suffered a sudden spell of dizziness so he stopped for a minute and rested his head between his legs.
Seeing this, a preppy Harvard student asked in very proper fashion, "Have you vertigo?"
The marathoner said, "Yes. Four more miles."

...

Sherlock Holmes and Dr. Watson were on a camping trip deep in the English countryside. They had retired for the evening and were lying there, looking up at the sky. Holmes said, "Watson, look up. What do you see?"
"Well, I see thousands of stars."
"And what does that mean to you?" said Holmes.
"Well, I guess it means we will have another fine day for the great outdoors tomorrow. What does it mean to you, Mr. Holmes?"
"To me, my dear Watson, it means someone has stolen our tent!"

I just love Chinese food. My favorite dish is number 27.
-Clement Attlee

ENTRÊES

God decides the world really needs another big flood so he goes and finds a descendant of Noah on Earth. "I need you to build an ark," God says to him. "You know the deal."

Noah's descendant nods. He spends a decade building his ark. The rain comes and pours for forty days and forty nights. When it finally ends, God is pleased that the ark remains intact. He tells Noah's great-great-great-great-great-great grandson to release all of the animals. "The what?" Noah's descendant asks.

"The animals in your ark," responds God.

"I don't have any animals. I'm a vegetarian," he says.

God is shocked and demands, "What do you have in there, then?"

"Two potatoes, two peas, two carrots…"

•••

Q: What did Roman nurses call IVs?

A: 4s

If you have formed the habit of checking on every new diet that comes along, you will find that, mercifully, they all blur together, leaving you with only one definite piece of information: french-fried potatoes are out. -Jean Kerr

Husband: How did the car wind up in the kitchen?

Wife: I made a left at the living room.

...

Two caterpillars are strolling along in the park when one sees a butterfly go by, points up at it and says to the other, "You'll never get me up in one of those things."

...

Albert walks into a podiatrist's office and says, "Doc, can you help me? I think I'm a moth."
The podiatrist says, "You don't need a podiatrist. You need a psychiatrist."
Albert responds, "Yeah, I know."
"Then why did you come in here if you need a psychiatrist?"
Albert answers, "Because the light was on."

...

Q: Why did the racehorse sneak behind the tree?

A: To change his jockeys

The only way to lose weight is to check it as airline baggage. -Peggy Ryan

ENTRÉES

A kangaroo escaped from the Bronx Zoo. After the zookeeper recaptured it, a 10-foot enclosure was put up. The next day, the kangaroo was on the loose again. After catching the marsupial again, a 20-foot high fence was made. Nonetheless, the kangaroo escaped the next morning. The frustrated zoo officials then constructed a fence 40 feet high. A camel occupying the enclosed area with the kangaroo said, "How much higher do you think they'll make this thing?"

The kangaroo said, "Who knows. This could go on forever if they don't remember to lock the gate."

≡ ≡

Two dogs are walking together on the side of the street. Suddenly, one dog says, "Just a second. I'll be right back." He walks over to the other side of the street and sniffs all around a fire hydrant. Then he comes back.

"What was that for?" asks his doggy pal.

"Oh, I was just checking my messages."

I hate brushing my teeth at night, because that means you can't have any more food and I'm hardly ever ready for that kind of commitment. -Robin Bienkowski

ENTRÉES

Three guys arrive at the Pearly Gates on Christmas Day and St. Peter is in a generous mood. "You may all enter Heaven provided you have something that represents this glorious holiday," St. Peter says with a smile.

The first guy pulls his car keys out of his pocket, jiggles them, and says, "The keys represent the bells of this wonderful holiday."

"You may go in," says St. Peter.

The next guy pulls out a penlight and says, "This represents the guiding light of the star of Bethlehem."

St. Peter signals him in with a sweep of his hand. The last guy is desperately searching through his pockets but all he can come up with is a pair of panties.

"And just what do those have to do with Christmas?" St. Peter thunders.

"Easy," replies the third guy with a nervous grin. "They're Carol's."

- - -

Then there was the paranoid dyslexic who always thought he was following someone.

They say that exercise and proper diet are the keys to a longer, healthier life. Watch for my next book, How I Died While Jogging. *-Drew Carey*

Woman: Doc, all spring and summer my husband has thought he's a lawn mower.

Doctor: My gosh! Why didn't you bring him here earlier?

Woman: Because my neighbor didn't return him until yesterday.

■ ■ ■

Boss: I've been reading that it's important to use humor at work to ease the tension, especially when there are job cutbacks. Knock-knock.

Employee: Who's there?

Boss: Not you anymore.

■ ■ ■

A guy goes to the circus and says to the ringmaster, "I do great bird impressions." The ringmaster says, "That's nothing special. Lots of people can do great bird impressions. Scram!" The guy says, "Okay," and flies away.

There's no better feeling in the world than a warm pizza box on your lap. -Kevin James

Slim Pickin's

"I spent my whole life trying to be thin just to find someone who'd love me once I got fat."
-Stephanie Klein

"Thin people are beautiful, but fat people are adorable." -Jackie Gleason

"I've exercised with women so thin that buzzards followed them to their cars."
-Erma Bombeck

Anonymous Musings:

If God wanted us to be thin, food wouldn't taste so good.

Skinny people are easier to kidnap. Stay safe, eat cake.

Unfortunately, my daydreams about being skinny are always interrupted by the sound of my own chewing.

When I buy cookies I eat just four and throw the rest away. But first I spray them with Raid so I won't dig them out of the garbage later. Be careful, though, because that Raid really doesn't taste that bad.
-Janette Barber

ENTRÉES

If you had to choose between eating bacon every day or being skinny for the rest of your life- would you choose Applewood or Hickory Smoked?

You're so slim that your mom actually enjoyed your birth.

You're so slim that you have to run around the shower to get wet.

You're so slim that you have to stand in the same place twice to cast a shadow.

You're so slim that you can hula-hoop with Cheerios.

Laughing Matters: Here's another important dietary benefit of this book- Reading alone burns 22 calories every 15 minutes.

A guy walks into a doctor's office with a carrot in his left ear, a banana in his right ear, and a cucumber up his nose. He says, "What's the matter with me, Doc?"
The doctor replies, "Well, for one thing, you're not eating properly."

Today, I bought cupcakes without sprinkles. Dieting is so hard. -Virginia Ward

A priest, a doctor and a lawyer were waiting to play golf and became frustrated with the slow play of the foursome ahead of them. "What's with these guys..." the lawyer grumbled. "We've been waiting to tee off at least 15 minutes."

"Here comes the greenskeeper," said the priest. "Let's have a word with him."

When confronted, the greenskeeper advised them that the slow-playing group were firefighters and that, sadly, they all lost their sight while saving the clubhouse from a fire a year ago. In gratitude, the club allowed them to play for free anytime.

The priest expressed his concern and said he'd keep them in his prayers, while the doctor volunteered to contact an ophthalmologist buddy to see if there was anything he could do for them.

The lawyer said, "Why can't these guys play at night?"

···

Patient: Doc, I have a terrible problem. I can't hold my water. I don't know when I'm gonna pee. What do I do?

Doctor: Get off my carpet.

I'm so hungry I could eat a vegetable. -Al Bundy, Married With Children

A guy goes to a store and asks a saleswoman for some help to buy his girlfriend a birthday gift. The saleswoman shows him a one hundred dollar bracelet. He says, "Way too much. What else have you got?"
She walks him over to the cosmetics counter, shows him a twenty-five dollar bottle of perfume and says, "How about this?"
"Nah, still too expensive. Can you show me something really cheap?"
She handed him a mirror.

* * *

A guy gets pulled over by a cop. The cop says, "How long have you been driving without a taillight, buddy?"
The guy yells, "Oh, no! Wait 'til my family finds out!"
The cop says, "Where's your family?"
"They're in the trailer that was hitched to my car!"

Q: Why are dogs such bad dancers?

A: They have two left feet.

Diet- Day 1 I have removed all the bad food from the house. It was delicious. -Rebekah Willey

The skydiving instructor is finishing up his first class and opens up the floor to questions. One of the students asks, "If my parachute doesn't open and the reserve chute doesn't work, how long will I have until I hit ground?"
The instructor replies, "You have the rest of your life."

. . .

Ollie and Ralph walk into a 7-11. A couple of minutes later they leave and Ralph says to Ollie, "Look at this," as he proudly produces three candy bars he's just stolen. "Pretty neat, huh," says Ralph.
"That's nothing," says Ollie. "Follow me."
They go back into the store and Ollie says to the cashier, "You wanna see a magic trick?"
"Sure, why not," responds the cashier.
Ollie promptly picks up a chocolate bar and eats it. Then he picks up another one and downs it. He takes one more candy bar and eats it.
The somewhat annoyed cashier says, "Where's the magic?"
Ollie points to Ralph and says, "Check his pockets."

There is no light so perfect as that which shines from an open fridge door at 2 a.m. -Nigel Slater

ENTRÉES

Bessie went into the bakery and asked how much the pastries cost.

"They're two for two dollars," said the store clerk.

"And how much for one?" asked Bessie.

"$1.25."

Bessie thought for a moment and said, "I'll take the other one."

* * *

A vacationer is taking an expedition through an African jungle when he asks the tour guide,

"Is this safe? I heard there are cannibals here."

The tour guide answers, "There are no cannibals in this particular jungle."

The vacationer says, "How can you be sure?"

The tour guide says, "We ate the last one Monday."

* * *

Bertha: That's the fourth time you've gotten up for the buffet. Aren't you embarrassed to be taking so many helpings?

Gus: Not at all. I keep telling everyone it's for you.

Tofu - What is that stuff? It's like chickpeas and grout. Food should not caulk windows. -Billiam Coronel

Grrrrroaners

Q: How do you make a dog disappear?

A: Use Spot remover.

...

Patient: Doc, I feel like a dog.

Doctor: How long have you felt this way?

Patient: Ever since I was a puppy.

...

A Golden Retriever and a Cocker Spaniel are out for a stroll. The Golden is upset and says, "My life is in shambles. I really need help." "How about going to see a shrink?" says the Spaniel. "I can't," responds the Retriever. "I'm not allowed on the couch."

...

It was so hot, a dog was seen chasing a cat and they were both walking.

My doctor told me to stop having intimate dinners for four - unless there are three other people.
-Orson Welles

ENTRÉES

Two fleas are outside the Empire State Building, heading up to New York's Central Park when one says to the other, "Shall we walk or take a dog?"

■ ■ ■

Q: What do you do with a broken dog?

A: Get him fixed.

■ ■ ■

In the old West one day, a Basset Hound hobbles into town with a heavily bandaged foot. The Dodge City sheriff says, "What's up, podna'?" The Basset answers, "I'm lookin' for the dog who shot my paw."

■ ■ ■

Then there was a dog that saw a sign, WET PAINT. He did.

■ ■ ■

Then there was the Pekingese dog that married a tomcat. Now they have a Peking Tom.

Rule #1 when dieting: If nobody sees you eating it, it doesn't contain any calories. -Joann Dolan

A fellow with a dog act goes to Hollywood for an interview with a talent agent. He brings his little Shitzu and St. Bernard into the agent's office. Right away, the Shitzu walks to the middle of the office floor and announces to the agent that he'd like to tell a few jokes. Following one hilarious joke after another, the agent says, "Wow, that Shitzu's unbelievable!"
The dog owner says, "The Shitzu's nothing. The St. Bernard is a ventriloquist!"

···

A pooch pays for a help wanted ad allowing for ten words. On the form, the dog fills out, "Woof, woof, woof, woof, woof, woof, woof, woof, woof."
The clerk takes a look at the ad and says, "You've only filled in nine words here. You're entitled to another woof for the same price." The dog answers, "But that would be silly."

Laughing Matters: Mayo Clinic nutrition experts say that laughter is like "internal jogging," temporarily increasing your heart rate and blood pressure, followed by muscle relaxation and a decrease in b.p.

I bought a talking refrigerator that said "Oink" every time I opened the door. It made me hungry for pork chops. -Marie Mott

"Congratulations, Norm!" said the TV game show host. "You've made it to the final round. Answer this two-part question on sports and you go home with a million dollars. Remember, Norm, the second question is always easier. Which part would you like first?"
Norm figured he'd play it safe and said, "I'll take the second part of the question first."
"Okay, Norm. Here it is - And in what year did it happen?"

...

Then there was the teacher who had a car accident. He was grading papers on a curve.

...

Muggsy pled guilty to auto theft and appeared before the judge in a packed courtroom.
"Why did you steal that car?" asked the judge.
"I had to get work," replied Muggsy.
"Couldn't you have taken the bus?" demanded the judge.
Muggsy answered, "I didn't have a driver's license for the bus."

Vegetables are a must on a diet. I suggest carrot cake, zucchini bread, and pumpkin pie. -Jim Davis

Stressed Spelled Backwards is Desserts

Don't forget, this is the reverse diet- the more you indulge, the less you bulge. Here, then, are some after dinner jokes for your consumption.

Harold went for a job interview. The boss asked him what he considered his biggest weakness. Harold said, "I'm brutally honest."
The boss said, "I don't think that's a weakness."
Harold replied, "I don't care what you think."

※ ※ ※

Hubbie: Hon, I'm calling you from the hospital. Gertrude brought me here. I had a horrible accident. They took X-rays. Both of my arms are broken and they don't know if they can save my left leg.

Wife: Who is Gertrude?

To diet: verb always used in the future tense.
-The Dieter's Dictionary

DESSERT

Knock-Knock

St. Peter says to God, "Look, Lord. I'm aware that you know everything, but if you want to appreciate a knock-knock joke, you gotta say, 'Who's there?'"

Knock-knock.
Who's there?
Spell.
Spell who?
Okay, W-H-O.

Knock-knock.
Who's there?
To.
To who?
No, it's to whom.

Knock-knock.
Who's there?
Short-term memory loss.
Short-term memory loss who?
Knock-knock.

If God did not intend for us to eat animals, then why did he make them out of meat? -John Cleese

DESSERT

Then there was the fellow who called the police about a murder on his front lawn. They said they couldn't do anything about the crows.

■ ■ ■

Fred was going on a blind date and was worried about what to do if he wasn't attracted to the girl. His buddy Arnold told Fred that there's an app for just such an occurrence. Arnold said, "It's called 'Mom are you okay?' and it schedules your cell phone to ring just after you meet your date. If you like her, just ignore the ring. If you don't, answer the phone and say, 'Mom? What's the matter? Are you okay?' It works every time. Trust me."

That night, Fred knocked on his blind date's door. She was drop dead gorgeous. Just as Fred was about to speak, the girl's phone rang. She answered it and said, "Mom? What's the matter? Are you okay?"

■ ■ ■

Q: What do you call a baby queen from England?

A: Lady Gaga

Exercise is a dirty word. Every time I hear it I wash my mouth out with chocolate. -Charles M. Schulz

Ethel was so disgusted with her husband, Wilbur, that she told him to get out. As he made his way toward the door she hollered, "I hope you die a very slow, painful death."
With that, Wilbur turned around and responded, "So, you want me to stay?"

■■■

A guy goes to a psychiatrist's office and says, "Doc, my wife is crazy. She thinks she's a chicken."
The shrink says, "Why don't you bring her in here?"
The guy answers, "I would, but we need the eggs."

■■■

Q: What do you call a guy who has gone AWOL on his diet?

A: A desserter

Q: What do you get from a North Pole cow?

A: Ice cream

Lord, if you can't make me thin - can you make all my friends fat? -Judy Hampton

DESSERT

Fred got stopped for speeding. The cop said, "Do you have any idea how fast you were going?"
Fred replied, "I was just trying to keep up with the traffic, officer."
The cop remarked, "There is no traffic, sir."
Fred said, "See how far behind I am?"

···

A golfer walks into the pro shop at the local course and asks if they sell ball markers. The cashier says they do, and they are a dollar apiece. The golfer gives the cashier a dollar. The cashier opens the register, puts the dollar in, and hands the golfer a dime.

···

Howard is having a beer at the bar with his friends. At one point, he sends a text to his wife. One of his pals pipes up, "What's the text say?"
Howard reads it out loud: "Having a beer with my buddies. If I'm not home in half an hour, read this text again."

Seize the moment. Remember all those women on the Titanic who waved off the dessert cart.
-Erma Bombeck

Oscar had a terrible mishap at the lumberyard as he pushed a tree through the buzz saw and accidentally sliced off all ten of his fingers. He rushed to the emergency room, where the doctor examined him and said, "No problem. With today's technology, I can reattach the fingers."

Oscar, in terrible pain, groaned, "But I don't have them."

The shocked doctor said, "Why not?"

Oscar moaned, "I couldn't pick them up."

...

A crowd of husbands are about to enter through the Pearly Gates when St. Peter roars, "Hold it right there! I want all of you who were henpecked husbands while on Earth to form a line to my right. The rest of you stand to my left."

All but one husband stands on the henpecked line. St. Peter turns to the guy standing alone and says, "How about you? What's your story?" He replies sheepishly, "My wife told me to stand here."

Strength is the ability to break a chocolate bar into four pieces with your bare hands - and then eat just one of the pieces. -Judith Viorst